THE **MEANINGFUL**
MODERN HOME

THE **MEANINGFUL** **MODERN** HOME

SOULFUL ARCHITECTURE AND INTERIORS

CELESTE ROBBINS
ROBBINS ARCHITECTURE

WRITTEN WITH JACQUELINE TERREBONNE
PRINCIPAL PHOTOGRAPHY BY ROGER DAVIES

Contents

Introduction

On a perfect spring day just outside Chicago, shortly after I completed ground-up construction of my own modern home, I opened my doors for a local house walk and welcomed a parade of curious visitors, neighbors wanting to peek inside and see how others in the community lived. Their reactions were wonderfully enthusiastic. They were transfixed by the wall of windows, stretching end to end across the rear facade, that showcased the sloping ravine in all its seasonal glory and brought the intoxicating beauty of a Midwest spring landscape into focus. The morning's display was a collage-like collection of vibrant new leaves with bright splashes of forsythia, animated by the movement of the sunlight filtering through the trees. To my delight, there was a kind of buzz, a sense of enchantment and surprise. The visitors, making their way through the house's open plan, expressed the same reactions again and again: "This home is so warm!" and "I didn't think that I was modern, but I could live here!" That's when I understood that I had captured something special, and that this vision of warm modernism—my own definition of modernism—would be my signature. It runs through all nine houses presented in this book, including two of my own homes.

When it comes to modern houses, many people assume that they could never live in a "glass box" without ever experiencing how gracious and meaningful it can feel. I did not set out to redefine modernism for myself and my clients, but after many years and many projects, I can now reflect on what it means to bring warmth, softness, and livability to modern design. Guided by principles rather than strict stylistic rules, my team at Robbins Architecture and I create inviting houses filled with personality, which translates into a true sense of home. I developed this approach by melding my personal philosophy with features central to historical modernism, such as open floor plans, connections to the surrounding landscape, and a clean aesthetic that emphasizes function and serenity over drama.

In my early training, I found inspiration in the work of Le Corbusier, Frank Lloyd Wright, and Rudolph Schindler. During my studies at Cornell University, I learned how these architects applied their own signatures to the tenets of modernism, and I came to understand the importance of clarity and conviction. Later, as I settled into my own architectural career in Chicago, I dived deeper into the local vernacular, discovering talents who artfully applied these ideas to the Midwestern landscape, and I've been lucky enough to live in homes designed by some of these greats.

From all these influences, I inherited a collection of principles that work together, such as how to use balance, proportion, and light to shape spaces and how to invite nature into the home.

To highlight the themes that define my studio's work, each chapter in this book reflects on a particular concept that creates modernism with meaning. I've built upon these lessons, learning to skillfully edit designs to create spaces so pure that the smallest, quietest details can reverberate. Sometimes I may leave a surface blank, because a white wall can become the perfect canvas for shadows and light as the day passes. Other times, I work hard to make the architecture virtually disappear, so that interior and exterior become one. The powerful details that I do incorporate, though, are ones that gracefully reveal a moment of artistry—whether it's a chiseled groove in an exterior stone wall, an illuminated reveal in the marble of a kitchen counter, or an unexpected cutout in a wooden stair rail. I relish knowing that these quietly potent details have an exponential impact on the overall design.

Balanced among these principles is something that typically goes unnoticed: the unseen rigor and resolution threaded through these homes. Precise alignments and thoughtful sequences guide you through a house like architectural choreography—leading you along repeated paths that over time bring resonance to the space.

To bring these domestic visions to life, I need the support of two critical groups—my clients and my team. My team and I embrace the complexity of decoding our clients' dreams and transforming those dreams into strong architectural ideas. Our clients' desires are the catalyst for creating unique, authentic houses, and that's proven by the range of styles in this book. Achieving any of this would be impossible without the talented team of like-minded artists that I have assembled at Robbins Architecture. They share my passion for bringing a home to life and life to a home. More than the open plans, the glass walls, and the response to the site, it's this passion that gives everything we create true, lasting meaning.

LAKESIDE
MIDCENTURY

Inspiration

For an architect, the world offers a constant stream of inspiration. Living within another architect's creation presents a unique influence: you feel and observe the soul of another's vision on an intimate level.

My first house was a midcentury modernist home built in 1938 by architect Henry Dubin, who was inspired by Frank Lloyd Wright's philosophy for congenial living. For years I lived within the warmth of his architectural expression: glass walls and deep roof overhangs brought nature into the home, while the open plan created a central gathering space with built-in nooks adding a complex layer of scales and experiences. Looking at my portfolio now, I can see the fingerprints of this home. The Dubin house had such an impact on me that when I discovered another midcentury gem, this one designed by Winston Elting, I instantly fell in love. The clear form of Elting's house sat in harmony with the lakeside landscape. It honored nature with its materials and design. I knew I could learn from its precise beauty while bringing my own voice to a renovation. While I respect midcentury design principles, I also wanted the house to feel fresh.

What I admired most about Elting's design was its utter simplicity. Although its plan is a rectangle of less than 3,000 square feet, it feels like so much more, embracing the two-and-a-half-acre property. The front of the house is a rigorous composition of brick walls and wood louvers, but the lakefront facade is completely transparent and opens to the sparkling water and soaring beech trees. That idea of transparency is knit throughout the house's interior, with a series of courtyards tucked into the layout. The homes I design tend to be more organic and complex in silhouette; Elting's house is the opposite, incorporating irregular cutouts into a neat box. Happily, that level of rigor doesn't leave the house bereft of quirky moments of nuance. They're integrated throughout the space, and it's a joy to spend time marveling at them.

But for all this house had to offer, updates were direly needed. It was important to me that the renovations were complementary to the house but not absolutely "period." I replaced the weathered and overworn wood with new Douglas fir, and swapped out the porcelain tile floors for wood. In the kitchen and bathrooms, I trusted my instincts and reshaped the design, knowing how closely aligned my aesthetic is to the home's vocabulary. I reconfigured the kitchen with shallow floor-to-ceiling storage. I added bifold pocket doors that hide the oven and cooktop, staying true to my belief that a kitchen should be more elegant than simply utilitarian. (I feel that Elting was guided by this spirit when he added the counter-height fireplace, which I now think of as the ultimate kitchen luxury.) In the bathrooms, I wrapped the shower walls and vanities with Four Seasons quartzite, which casts a pink glow. This rosy tone became a soft and unexpected layer that I used as a color motif throughout.

Ultimately, this project felt like a collaboration across the decades. The more time I spend in this home, the more I soak in its beauty and intelligence. By living within the space, I've had time to study and appreciate the subtleties of its design. And already I can see the house influencing my other projects. The enchantment continues, and I am certain it will inform my work for years to come.

PAGES 12–13: The simple grid structure, accommodating a linear arrangement of rooms enjoying views to the lake, extends beyond the exterior walls, reinforcing the clarity of the plan.

PAGE 14: Rounding a corner, one discovers the house's glassy entryway, which gives a clear view through the living area to the lake.

PREVIOUS: I designed the interiors to complement the house's Douglas fir envelope with layers of art, furniture, and objects in various types of warm wood.

RIGHT: Interiors and architecture unite to create warmth and lightness.

OPPOSITE: The custom-designed wood console has an irregular, organic shape that is distinguished by its dark chocolate stain. A 1950s wall sculpture by an Italian artist echoes its rounded edges.

RIGHT: To add interest and texture, I topped the table with a vintage Scandinavian runner and a collection of ceramics in a variety of glazes.

OVERLEAF: During the restoration process, I took care to maintain the home's midcentury modern spirit in the interiors. Bold but comfortable furniture with cozy textures is both simpatico with this character and highly livable for today.

PREVIOUS: In the seating area of the great room, a fireplace in rosy Chicago brick in an inventive pattern creates an interesting moment that contrasts with the wood of the interior architecture. I selected vintage Guillerme et Chambron chairs, plush ottomans (used as a cocktail table), and repurposed Scandinavian textiles on the pillows to add both softness and personality.

ABOVE AND OPPOSITE: Textural details and treasured objects create warmth and interest throughout the home. These types of curated vignettes give the interiors a contemporary flair.

PAGE 26: In a corner of the great room, I placed a second table (this one by Guillerme et Chambron) for morning coffee, reading books, and doing puzzles.

PREVIOUS: In a surprising architectural gesture, built-in shelves displaying an ever-changing array of art, ceramics, and fresh flowers extend across a vertical slot window.

LEFT: Hiding the appliances conceals the functionality of the Boffi kitchen, transforming the room into another beautiful place to gather. The inventive mix of materials, including marble countertops and backsplash and brick walls, departs from the wood theme seen throughout the rest of the house.

BELOW: A fireplace in the kitchen is an unexpected luxury.

OPPOSITE: A view from the great room into the office provides a glimpse into one of the courtyards. Toni Zuccheri wall lights are artworks in themselves.

ABOVE AND RIGHT: Opposite the front door, a lounge seat, accompanied by a Charles Zana lamp, enjoys a prime view of an interior courtyard, which can be closed off for privacy with patterned ivory sheers. Dark wood shelves, continuing the language of the great room, are lightened by a backing of coral linen.

RIGHT: This modestly sized guest bedroom provides cozy charm and a meditative view of the courtyard, with plantings by Scott Byron & Co.

LEFT AND BELOW: In a second guest bedroom that overlooks the lake, a headboard upholstered with a woven rug adds character. I added other warm elements, including a Robert Kime pillow, circa 1950 Swedish lamps, a Rosemary Hallgarten throw, and sheepskin-covered chairs.

OVERLEAF: Since the primary bedroom, which has both lakeside and courtyard views, is positioned at one end of the house, pinkish brick forms one of the walls. A mohair-upholstered chair was inspired by the building material's blush hues, while on the pillows subtly embroidered fabric from Chelsea Textile enlivens the bed linens.

PAGES 40–41: From day to night, the house transforms, in the evening beaming like a lantern atop the hill.

MOUNTAIN
MODERN

Connectivity

When designing a house on a vast, eighty-nine-acre parcel of land surrounded by the Rocky Mountains, uniting that home with its magnificent surroundings is a primary objective. But for a home to be truly successful, a feeling of connection needs to run even deeper—encouraging kinship among those inside and nature outside.

The depth of these internal and external connections is clear as soon as you approach the house, with its long site wall that draws you into the entry courtyard. Here the roof extends with a dramatic cantilever and the home envelops you; this first outdoor "room" of the house greets you before you even enter, establishing a soft edge between indoors and out. By creating spaces that both thread nature through the home, and that bring people together, such as the outdoor dining area nestled below a fourteen-foot overhang off the kitchen, the house conveys a feeling of intimacy that complements the expansive site.

The joyful dance between the power of the mountains and the delicacy of the valley grasses inspired the design. To give the house scale and strength, we chose concrete as one of the main materials. Pulling inspiration from the Clyfford Still Museum, by Allied Works, in nearby Denver, we designed the facade with vertical board-formed concrete, which created a beautiful textured pattern that harmonizes with the snowy peaks. Horizontal boards would have been easier to execute, but the vertical language better balanced the home's substantial proportions and rooflines.

In contrast to the strong concrete facades, walls of glass appear impossibly thin and light, seeming to gracefully disregard the weight of the masses above. These transparent planes guide you through the house: the front door, a five-foot-wide sliding pane of glass, is an almost invisible separation that beckons you inside; the effect is reversed in the great room, which features an expansive thirty-two-foot-wide glass wall that is motorized to open the room to the dazzling vistas and crisp air. The dialogue between the powerful tectonic forms of the concrete and the delicacy of the glass brings a complex shift of scales in keeping with the mountain landscape.

To complement the palette of glass and concrete, we introduced a warm layer of dark stained oak. The richness of the wood brings character and animation to the underside of the roof overhangs. This same stained oak also graces the interior, including the architectural wall that backs the seating area and directs circulation with its implied edge.

But the grandest gesture, by far, is the double-height wall that provides a backdrop for the stair, of which each tread seems to float, maintaining sight lines to the mountain-peak view. An integral part of its design, the stair anchors the home with nature's own design language of delicacy and strength. This sculptural stair is a bold move that connects the architecture to the powerful natural landscape that surrounds the house.

PREVIOUS: A beautiful tension is created by having the glassy transparent first floor support the largely concrete-clad second floor, while the roof cantilevers over the structure to shelter an entryway that welcomes visitors from the vast landscape.

LEFT: Continuous windows and sliding pocket doors provide a delicate edge between inside and out, with a rhythm that establishes a sense of movement throughout the home's open layout.

49

RIGHT: The entryway gradually draws visitors inside by removing distinctions between interior and exterior. A grassy courtyard with carefully placed trees reinforces the sense of space and beauty.

OVERLEAF: A motorized thirty-two-foot window wall disappears, opening the great room to the landscape.

OPPOSITE: In order to dissolve the distinction between indoor and outdoor, interior designer Shawn Henderson conceived seating areas that make the most of the dramatic views for entertaining and relaxing.

BELOW: A room isn't always defined by four walls. This floating panel of cerused oak suggests space without dictating function, and it references the golden onyx freestanding wall in Mies van der Rohe's iconic Barcelona Pavilion.

LEFT: The open floor plan accommodates a dining table that serves many functions. Enlivening the architecture with furnishings gives a sense of purpose to the layout, with the view forming the perfect backdrop.

BELOW: An arrangement of local pottery adds an artistic moment without feeling fussy.

ABOVE: The kitchen was designed so that appliances almost disappear. Materials such as black limestone and cerused oak add atmosphere.

OPPOSITE: A center island provides both storage and seating, creating a place to eat, cook, gather, and take in a view of the pool.

OVERLEAF: To realize stairs that look this ethereal is a feat of engineering. By hiding the structure and using a zigzag stringer, the suspension of the flights seems effortless.

PAGE 61: Upstairs, the scale becomes more intimate. Cerused wood and white walls combine to bring a brightness to the traditional concept of a mountain home that feels fresh and modern.

PREVIOUS: Thoughtfully furnished terraces blur the transition from indoors to the natural landscape. The site's initial composition of hardscape and native plants was designed by Hoerr Schaudt, with further plantings added by Design Workshop.

LEFT: At dusk, the harmony between indoors and out becomes more apparent, especially with the windows pocketed away. Outside, the warmth of the wood slat overhang balances the poured concrete flooring, while inside the envelope is mellow and serene.

OVERLEAF: The house is anchored into the vastness of the landscape by a site wall that extends along the driveway. The scale of the house is humanized by breaking the functions of the home into multiple smaller structures.

HOME ON
THE RANCH

Warmth

Wrapped with wood both inside and out, this ranch-inspired retreat near Jackson Hole, nestled in the valley of the Teton Mountains, exudes a special kind of warmth. This house was my first ground-up project and marks the beginning of my firm. At the time, I was working from my home with no associates, and as a result, I poured all of myself into the design—obsessing over every tiny detail. As I visualized each space coming to life on paper, I knew this project was a remarkable opportunity. With the jagged mountain peaks as a backdrop and richly colored horses roaming the sage landscape, this Western scene was an ideal place to create a retreat from urban life for the owners. The resulting home met their needs in such an authentic and absolute fashion that they eventually made it their permanent residence.

To maximize the stunning views while creating harmony within the setting, I sought to strike a balance between the vocabulary of the ranches that dot the Wyoming landscape and a modernist architectural lexicon. From a distance, the house fits within its surroundings with a characteristic mountain vernacular and a familiar sense of scale. However, a closer look reveals that it has more than a traditional Western aesthetic. A composition of flat roofs is decidedly modern, but it is always in dialogue with the familiar gabled roof peaks of its neighbors. In the great room, a wall of windows extends edge to edge to capture the unparalleled view. This dramatic gesture, rooted in modernism, ties the home visually to Grand Teton as it brings the mountains' powerful silhouettes inside.

It may have been a subconscious lesson, but this site taught me the importance of connecting a home more deeply with nature while creating warm and inviting places to gather. I was able to create intimate moments within the vastness of the open valley by carving out exterior living spaces, shaping outdoor rooms with fireplaces to assemble around as well as a trellised terrace for dining. Creating opportunities for family and friends to be together approaches the true purpose of a home like this.

I designed the home with a grand living space that provides a setting for dining and ample fireplace seating—a perfect place to host a large, convivial group. But as the owners wanted the house to be just as meaningful after their children moved away, I also provided smaller furniture groupings within the larger room to ensure that the house would feel cozy for just the two of them.

I set out to design a home with a timeless elegance—to create a home that welcomes all that its stunning site has to offer into the context of this family's lifestyle. Now, with the wisdom of experience, I know that this is what brings design to life. The result is a home that reflects how the owners dreamed of living—warmly and with meaningful connections to the things, people, and places that are important to them.

PREVIOUS: To capture the spectacular view, we kept the house as transparent as possible, with broad windows—inspired by those at the Schindler House in Los Angeles—with proportions highlighting the horizon line. Additionally, the rhythm of the mullions extends to the adjacent bookshelves, creating a calming sense of unity.

OPPOSITE: Berta Shapiro's thoughtfully furnished interiors include back-to-back blue sofas in the great room, which create smaller conversation areas.

ABOVE AND RIGHT: Nature is brought into the house in the detailing of the furniture, including accent tables in rugged but refined materials.

RIGHT: The fireplace—a focal point of the great room—floats in the space, rather than dividing it.

OVERLEAF: Log storage is built into the mantel, and the library is tucked around the corner.

PAGE 81: In contrast to the expansive great room, the library is intimate. Architectural details such as the window frames and hardware are consistent throughout the home and impactful in rooms of different scales.

LEFT: Harmonious wood tones make for a clean, inviting kitchen, perfect both for cooking and for entertaining.

BELOW: Earthy accent bowls filled with fruit bring color and life to the space.

RIGHT: From the outdoor terrace only, the horizontal line of the roof is visible. This detail brings the vastness of the landscape down to a human scale.

MIDWEST SANCTUARY

Artistry

For me, every decision that shapes a home comes back to artistry. An asymmetrical roofline, a groove carved into a stone facade, the interplay of materials—all these elements speak to the fundamental artistic principles of proportion, balance, and light.

For this summer home, situated on a golf course in the north suburbs of Chicago, we integrated artistry at all scales. When designing a home, the first artistic gesture is to sculpt the overall form. Long rooflines balance the home's strong proportions. Outdoor spaces are crafted to bring families together with nature as a focal point. In this project, we brought to life a grand outdoor room that became the heart of the home, a courtyard that celebrates the Midwestern summer centered around swimming and golf.

But artistry doesn't only come with such grand moves. Throughout this home, small-scale touches foster an appreciation for the talented hands that bring these expressions to life. Extraordinary craftspeople were commissioned to create custom design elements in metal, glass, and stone. These specially crafted details bring intimate moments to counterbalance the broad expanses of glass and the monolithic exterior walls clad in Ramon gray limestone that define the house's envelope. The fossil-imprinted stone, for example, infuses a layer of time and scale between the modern glass walls, but I took the human connection even further by introducing hand-chiseled vertical recesses to the facade. This is not a "form follows function" moment; it's a soulful, personal touch that brings to life what modernism is to me.

Sometimes a technical challenge sparks artistry. One of the main drivers of this project was the owner's request for uninterrupted views of the pool and golf course. To accomplish this, we shifted the structural columns to the exterior of the glass facade. As a result, the windows appear whisper-thin from the inside, while on the exterior, the blackened steel columns add texture and definition to the covered walkway that connects the volumes of the house.

The significance of craftmanship is picked up once again in small backlit light follies in the countertop of the kitchen's organically shaped island, which was inspired by the curves of an Alvar Aalto vase. Instead of being a workhorse surface, it takes on the sensuous quality of a sculpture. The kitchen range hood is a subtle yet rich composition of metal, stone, and glass that combines materiality and illumination to bring another artistic element to the interior.

Artistry became our solution whenever we encountered a functional need. Instead of a task to accomplish, my team and I took it as an opportunity to celebrate craft and design.

PAGE 90: A gap between the roof overhang and the house allows light to filter into the great room.

LEFT: In the great room, interior designer Janet McCann defined small seating groupings that make the space more intimate. Outside, the pool is set eighteen inches below, so that it is obscured by plantings in summer and disappears into the landscape during the winter months. Mariani Landscape Design created a composition of plants that is stunning year round.

OPPOSITE: Doors of ribbed glass and patinated steel pocket into the wall except for a section of glass and metal, which remains exposed.

RIGHT: A finely detailed stair is another of the many artistic elements in this house.

OVERLEAF: A fireplace with a unique floor-to-ceiling, glass-and-metal surround anchors the great room. Beyond, doors open to the terrace.

PREVIOUS: At one end of the great room, a lounge with a seating area and a custom bar form a natural spot for entertaining family and friends alike.

BELOW: Illuminated glass reveals in the kitchen island bring an unexpected moment of modern glamour.

RIGHT: The sculptural marble-topped bar was the fulfillment of the client's request for a large kitchen island with an irregular shape.

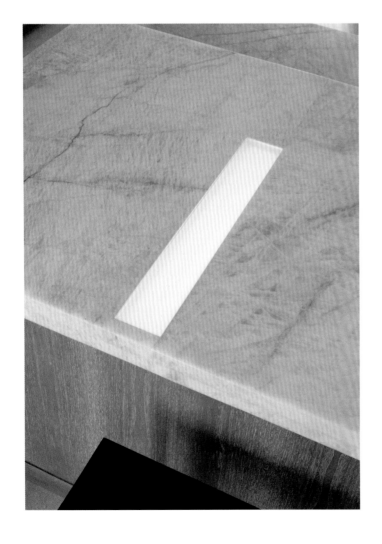

PREVIOUS: Even a range hood can become a moment of architectural expression. Taking its cues from the fireplace in the great room, the hood features a graphic composition of glass and steel panels.

RIGHT: The primary bath features his-and-hers sinks and closets flanking each side. On the left, toilets and a shower are separated by glass walls framed in bronze.

OPPOSITE: The pool runs parallel to the great room but is removed enough to give each space an air of intimacy. That separation is further highlighted by changes in material and elevation: the ipe deck sits eighteen inches lower than the terrace adjacent to the house.

RIGHT: The clients appreciate thoughtful details that bring craft to the modernist architecture, such as this hand-chiseled detail on the exterior facade.

OVERLEAF: Wrapping the house around the courtyard creates distinct zones for different functions and levels of privacy, while allowing views of the terrace from almost every room.

WESTERN

RETREAT

Balance

Balance is central to all aspects of design. Sometimes balance presents itself in the power and resolve of symmetry. Sometimes it is less obvious, and the only signal of its presence is a feeling of peace. Sitting within the sleepy town of Driggs, Idaho, our "Western Retreat" begins with balance. After ascending "the pass," a steep and winding mountain road, the hustle and bustle of Jackson Hole gives way to a dreamy valley landscape—grassy fields, blue skies, and mountain silhouettes. Nature has no trouble creating balance. Shape, line, form, and palette unite at all scales, from the delicate intricacy of the aspen leaf to the tapestry of the valley wetlands at the foot of the jagged peaks.

This landscape is my inspiration. With the Tetons as a backdrop, pitched roofs over the two main volumes of the house nod to the regional architectural vernacular. Then, our signature modernist flat roof is applied to announce the entry and, beneath it, a wide wall of windows. This is where the art and soul of the design surfaces. When I work with these shapes, I feel like a sculptor molding the subconscious balance of wall to window, or in architect-speak "solid-void." The overall effect is subtle in its presentation.

But a house is more than a series of forms. Just as essential are the materials that give this retreat character. Interpreting the regional palette of metal roofs and cedar walls, I've conjured them into something quite different. There's the lightness provided by the large panels of glass that punctuate the house and animate the facades. Sometimes these moments provide a peek at the interior; at other times, the glass instead frames a dazzling view straight through the house to the vista beyond. In that way, the architecture is vitally connected to the landscape. With windows that extend right across a wall, you are totally immersed in the valley, even when you're inside. But there's a sense of order that gently controls the interaction.

Ultimately, all of these complementary features come together to produce a home that's familiar and welcoming—yet strong and architectural. Its quiet confidence is palpable the instant the rooflines come into sight, and even more powerful from within each room in the house. By perfectly tying together proportions, materials, and connections to the outdoors, we have created a house that achieves a clear and harmonious equilibrium between man and nature.

PAGES 116–17: The flat roof of the transparent connector that defines the entryway creates a beautiful sense of balance between this home's two pitched-roof volumes. The house's landscape was designed by Design Workshop.

PAGE 118: In the entryway, a humble but beautifully crafted table and stools quietly coexist with the rigorously edited architectural detailing. Minimalist furnishings complement the large panes of the windows and doors.

RIGHT: With towering windows and tall glass doors, the great room feels immersed in the outdoors.

ABOVE AND OPPOSITE: Metal accents in the great room—including a chandelier custom designed by the interior designer Herringbone Design, the detailing of the rafters, and decorative accessories—are both elegant and suitably rustic.

OPPOSITE: A large clean-lined dining table encourages lingering without distracting from the spectacular view.

RIGHT: Local millworkers endowed the oak cabinets, and their minimal detailing and chicken wire fronts, with efficient beauty.

BELOW: Chic wall lights evoking candle sconces, also by Herringbone Design, would be at home in a city apartment but are equally appropriate in this Western retreat.

RIGHT: A backsplash of blue Heath tiles and a patinated-steel range hood create a warm dialogue with the great room fireplace on the opposite wall.

PAGE 129: For a client who enjoys cooking, a view from the kitchen out to the terrace and to nature was critical.

OPPOSITE AND ABOVE: Placing the terrace dining table on axis with the kitchen doorway creates an indoor-outdoor enfilade.

RIGHT: Pressing aspen leaves into the still-wet surface of the poured-concrete table created an everlasting impression.

RIGHT: At one end of the house, a door sheltered by an overhang leaves open the possibility of adding another wing or guest quarters in the future.

OVERLEAF: The horizontal board-formed concrete of the outdoor fireplace contrasts with the vertical wood planks of the house's exterior walls. The neutral palette recedes and allows the greens and yellows of the grasses to take center stage.

OPPOSITE: The primary bedroom opens directly to the landscape. It was important that the private rooms have the same connection with nature as the communal spaces.

BELOW: A Holly Hunt occasional table complements the textures and materials that give the house its character.

RIGHT: A guest bedroom has a calming neutral palette that allows the view to come to the fore.

OVERLEAF: The vanity in the primary suite bath continues the language of the kitchen cabinetry but is topped by a Calacatta gold marble counter. The fixtures, hardware, and mirror details all relate back to the blackened steel window frames.

PAGE 141: The primary bedroom boasts a handsome custom platform bed. Knotted wood lends the piece a rugged warmth, while the upholstered, metal-trimmed headboard is undeniably sophisticated.

PAAVO TYNELL

ABOVE: Multiple flat-roofed connectors between the pitched-roof masses bring a pleasingly human scale to the house. The material language of metal and glass and the vertical lines connect these volumes to each other.

OVERLEAF: From a distance, the house evokes the local vernacular, and the choice of materials allows it to blend into the landscape. Only once one gets a closer look do the modernist touches reveal themselves.

INTO THE WOODS

Inside Out

Each site has a story, and from the first schematic sketch, a home's design is informed by its surroundings. Some sites are vast and open, while others are more intimate in scale. When I designed this house on the North Shore of Chicago for my family, I was inspired by the location's magnificent natural formations and let the tree-layered ravine with its intermittent stream guide my vision. Following a modernist principle of honoring nature, I brought the outside in and the inside out.

From early in the design process, I knew I wanted the same handsome wood window frames for this project that I had used on other projects. I had fallen in love with their bold, blocky design and beautiful natural character. That decision was the foundation for a lexicon of stained wood panels that appear throughout the exterior and interior of the house. While architects often bring the rustic look of exterior woodwork inside, I did the opposite, applying the precision of cabinetry to the outside panels. After much experimentation and determination, this look was precisely engineered in the same way that a yacht is built.

A graceful dialogue between indoors and outdoors nurtures a feeling of being utterly surrounded by the landscape. Where the ravine crosses the property, it creates a level, grassy area that drops off into a thick, steep woodland. That duality sparked the concept of creating two separate moods within the main communal areas of the house. The living room is very much an expression of the ravine: moody and cozy with a large fireplace, handsome wood paneling, and a notable collection of midcentury furniture, bounded on one side by an entire wall of glass. This segment of the house is sited on the edge of the forested slope, and the room feels engulfed in branches and the patterning of the trees.

In contrast, the kitchen, which overlooks the sunny lawn, is bright and light, with white cabinetry. As a mother, I wanted this room to be inviting, so I also made it a circulation space, and in many ways it acts more as a family room than as a kitchen. Outside the kitchen, the terrace functions as another gathering space. Adjacent to the terrace is one of my favorite features—the infinity-edge reflecting pool filled with swimming koi and flowering lily pads.

By creating this home for myself and my family, I was able to bring to life my personal design philosophy that drawing the intrinsic beauty of nature into the home is essential. This house became a calling card, and clients who experienced it have asked for me to imbue their own homes with the same sensibility. For the last decade and a half, the house has not only been a home but also the foundation of my practice.

PREVIOUS: As you arrive at this house, the flat roofline establishes a comfortable domestic scale and offers a view straight through the house. The exterior oak paneling resembles interior millwork in its refined execution.

RIGHT: To maximize the impact of the ravine view, the window mullions in the great room are organized in an irregular rhythm to frame the natural groupings of trees.

OVERLEAF: The mix of furniture I selected—including an armchair by Alvar Aalto, at left; a 1950s Italian chair; and a carved-wood midcentury lamp—reflects my deep appreciation for design. The coffee table showcases favorite curiosities, including small metal figures—three-dimensional "doodles" made from leftover foundry scraps—found at an antique show.

OPPOSITE: In the great room, industrial metal legs on the dining table contrast nicely with the abundance of wood. A tabletop lamp encourages reading, puzzle-making, and other activities, as well as sharing meals.

ABOVE: I filled a shelf with books and treasures to make the upstairs hallway feel more like a room than merely a place to pass through.

OVERLEAF: The long kitchen table is a kind of hub. Bench seating runs end to end, accommodating family and friends for casual dinner parties; it also serves as a great place to hang out, do homework, and keep the cook company.

BELOW AND RIGHT: I decorated the television room with a mix of sculptural but soft-edged furniture, including a side table by Charles Dudouyt, which adds character with its unexpected base.

LEFT: A koi pond transforms the outdoor space with the beauty of lily pads and the sound of water. Wood paneling on the garage makes this functional structure a suitable backdrop for the pond and the adjacent bed of decorative grasses.

163

OPPOSITE: A balcony that runs across the second story reduces the scale of the home and provides a lookout from the kids' bedrooms. Below, outdoor furniture is placed to the side to avoid blocking views from the interior.

RIGHT: The consistent language of wood windows and doors creates harmony throughout the house.

OVERLEAF: The stairs seem to float when viewed from the entry, offering a view to the koi pond. Everything unfolds in a carefully orchestrated sequence. At the top of the stairs, a bridge connects sections of the second floor.

PAGE 167: The strong contrast between the rich dark tone of the wood and the white stucco walls enlivens the landing.

RIGHT: I filled the interiors with modern pieces that felt at home with the woodland site. A large Japanese screen from the 1950s has the same depth as the views outside. The two smaller artworks are ink drawings by Alfonso Iannelli.

BELOW AND RIGHT: A continuous ribbon of glass spans one wall of the bath, offering a beautiful seasonal view out into the treetops. A suspended mirror separates the dressing room from the wet area.

ABOVE: Water lilies in the koi pond provide ever-changing life to the landscape, which was designed in collaboration with Scott Byron & Co.

OPPOSITE: As one moves up the stairs, a dance with the landscape unfolds: the entry level looks out across the koi pond; the landing gives a view into the trees; and the bridge at the second floor overlooks the ravine.

MAKING
WAVES

Context

On the southwest shore of Lake Michigan, about three hours from Chicago, is a vacation community where generations gather each year for time at the beach, working on crafts, playing tennis, and enjoying live music. My client's family had grown up summering there in "the Cottage," which suited them perfectly for many years. Now, with a family of his own, the sleeping porch with twin beds and the dormer became too tight, and he and his wife began looking for opportunities to expand. Properties in this community rarely become available, so they jumped at the chance to buy a small lakefront site that was nestled between neighboring cottages. Even though it had very little acreage, I knew this would be a special project. The same family that had brought me the "Home on the Ranch" project in Jackson Hole were now looking for an entirely different vision of life.

As we had in Wyoming, we approached this project by relying on a foundation of modernist principles, while aiming for entirely different results. At first glance, the home fits quietly among the neighboring cottages by using local vernacular materials and forms: cedar shingles, tongue-and-groove accents, and a pitched roof. Yet upon closer study, tucked under the roof eave, a flat roof addition provides a crisp, modern edge for our signature wall of windows.

Unlike many of my projects, which spread out into vast landscapes, this site was limited by its modest size and steep slope. We responded by keeping the layout simple and taking advantage of the topography to capture the dramatic horizon line of the lake. Approaching the house, large, roughly cut limestone steps lead to the front door. Upon entering, the first view is of the built-in dining nook, a welcoming and cozy invitation. Configured more tightly than the Wyoming home, the great room, accommodating areas for living and dining as well as the kitchen, anchors the communal spaces and looks out to the lake view. Since the site is on a substantial hill that pitches up and then drops nearly twenty feet to the water, we devised a facade made almost entirely of glass, conjuring the impression that the waves roll right up to the windows. And so, the intimate interior space expands to take in the sweeping view of Lake Michigan; the sparkle and movement of the water are a constant presence in the home.

Thoughtful interior selections, including custom ceramic pendant lights over the kitchen island, a cornflower-blue velvet-upholstered chair, and a stunning 1938 tapestry, enliven the space and echo the colors and light of the sky and lake. A double-sided limestone fireplace divides the common area and the more private sitting room, which is lined with bifold doors that open to nature. That connection to the outside continues throughout the home, allowing it to expand beyond its edges and give new meaning to its tight site. Whether it's framing an expansive mountain view or the rolling waves of a lake, modern architecture sets the stage and lets nature take the lead.

PREVIOUS: Landscape architects Hoerr Schaudt collaborated on the design of the terrace, which features an irregular paving pattern and brings greenery right up to the house. The steel window frames, flat roofline, and shingles feel at home with the vernacular of this beach community.

ABOVE: The casual character of the neighborhood called for a modest front door. Instead of a grand entry hall, visitors are greeted with a welcoming dining area within the great room.

OPPOSITE: Patterned fabric wall covering extends to line the bookcase, lending a sense of color and texture to the dining area. We added Charlotte Perriand chairs, a custom banquette with storage below, and a Noguchi lantern to complete the family-friendly nook.

RIGHT: Seen from the great room, the lake seems to roll right up to the house.

185

RIGHT: Bifold doors open the living area to the outdoors. Furniture from the 1930s complements our custom-designed organically shaped coffee table.

OVERLEAF: A pretty detail cut into the newel post lends a freshness that enhances the lighthearted feel of the home.

PAGE 189: A hallway adjacent to the kitchen, decorated with an artwork by Milton Avery and a Scandinavian rug, functions as a mudroom with the requisite bench, hooks, and cubbies.

PAGES 190–91: In the primary bedroom, a long window seat with concealed storage is both cozy and functional.

TRIBECA
LOFT

Viewpoint

In my designs, which often feature a strong connection to the outdoors, sight lines always play an important role in the overall composition. Views can comprise a quiet, natural backdrop or, as in the case of this loft in New York's Tribeca neighborhood, a cacophony of rooftops, and each project is unique and calls for its own relationship to its surroundings. Originally renovated by Japanese architect Shigeru Ban, the home's massive windows frame a complex array of water towers, cast-iron facades, and the buzzy street life below. In response, we created a peaceful retreat with thoughtfully conceived interiors rendered in a soothing neutral palette. There is skill in editing a design so that each gesture has purpose. Simplicity is harder than it looks, but if done successfully, it can generate an elegant dialogue with a vibrant urban tapestry.

For their family of four, my clients wanted the kitchen to be open yet also have a sense of privacy. Balancing these opposing directives was initially a challenge, but the creative solution that resulted was both innovative and beautiful: playing off the midcentury strategy of integrating hanging kitchen storage, we devised a shelving unit suspended from the ceiling that divides the cooking area from the dining area. When illuminated, it emits a soft glow that transforms what is essentially functional into a decorative lantern over the island work surface. Extending beyond this divider, the island offers a more intimate and less formal place for eating, homework, and other daily activities.

Creating small-scale moments within a large, open space became a theme repeated in the primary bedroom suite, which we reconfigured to meet our clients' specific requests. Unlike many renovations that call for knocking down walls, here the goal was to carve out smaller, cozier areas. We added a vertical divider with pocket doors that slide out of each side to define an intimate sitting room off the bedroom for watching television, catching up on emails, or doing some late-night reading. Custom shelving backed with silk mohair by interior designer Mary Luby adds a sense of luxury to this purposely diminutive space.

Aside from the primary suite and kitchen reconfigurations, the owner wished for the home to exhibit a sense of personal and artistic expression in keeping with her family's legacy of originality and creativity. We brought character and detailing to the design with subdued but impactful materials such as the fluted marble in the powder room. With a soft palette of whites and neutrals, lighting accents were integrated in unexpected ways throughout the loft, adding an important and nuanced layer to the design. The serene space that emerged satisfied the family's unique vision for their home and their lives within the fabric of their city.

PAGE 196: A casual seating area invites visitors into the loft's great room.

PREVIOUS: The double-height loft has a balcony overlooking the living area. The client wanted the space to be light, bright, and white. Interior designer Mary Luby curated a collection of interesting furnishings to invigorate the subtle envelope.

ABOVE: A free-form stone-stopped table by Vincenzo De Cotiis creates interest while staying within the soothing, neutral palette.

OPPOSITE: A wall sculpture by Andrew Lord surmounts a console by Vincenzo De Cotiis.

RIGHT: The open floor plan creates an easy flow from the dining area to the sunny kitchen, with its connection to the outdoor terrace.

OPPOSITE: The orientation of the kitchen highlights the characteristic windows of this Tribeca building, which was originally renovated by architect Shigeru Ban.

OVERLEAF: Suspended shelving creates an airy separation between the kitchen and the dining area and becomes a light box when illuminated in the evenings. Appliances are for the most part concealed, eliminating visual clutter.

RIGHT: An additional seating area, with artwork by Christopher Wool, is inviting without being overly casual.

art piece
to replace
hallway shadow
box

LEFT: A large canvas by Vivian Suter introduces a calming palette to the primary bedroom. During the renovation, the entire suite was reconfigured to create smaller, cozier spaces in what had previously been one large room.

OVERLEAF: Floor-to-ceiling openings can be closed off with pocket doors to separate the bedroom from the sitting room.

PAGE 213: The sitting room features soft color and plenty of texture, with pink silk mohair backing the bookcases. Darrell Hawthorne, of Architecture & Light, devised a lighting scheme that emits a warm glow.

ABOVE AND OPPOSITE: The powder room—an exercise in minimalism—is energized by the undulating curve of a wall sheathed in fluted marble.

RAVINE
RETREAT

Intuition

Designing a house should not be a theoretical exercise. While there are technical challenges to solve, a home is born, not from checklists and spreadsheets, but from a meditative place where intuition shapes something uniquely special. The owner of this house in a Chicago suburb had seen my own home and wanted theirs to have the same clean lines, the same relationship to the environment, and the same warm atmosphere for their family, which includes two young girls.

The home stretches across its narrow site, embracing the natural beauty of the ravine landscape with its networks of streams and engaging expansive views that include a sliver of Lake Michigan in the winter months when trees are bare. These open views were not an option on the street-facing elevation, however, which needed to serve the more practical purpose of privacy. There, a long Indiana limestone wall, beneath a deep canopy, is articulated by a series of solid limestone piers that create a rhythm across the facade and, like the trees in the forest, filter atmospheric light between their vertical forms. We repeated this strategy throughout the home's exterior with syncopated panels of large-format, 2¼-inch-thick limestone placed at varying widths.

Once inside, a circulation path along the perimeter of the house provides ample wall space for the clients' impressive and ever-growing art collection. But the big reveal comes with the rooms facing the ravine. Their floor-to-ceiling sliding glass doors and equally expansive windows give the sensation of soaring through the treetops. A slight shift in the otherwise rectilinear plan angles a section of the house, including the primary bedroom, toward the glimmering lake.

By shaping the indoor and outdoor spaces in tandem, the house can function and flow seamlessly between inside and out. The home is anchored on one end by the formal living space, where the owners can entertain guests and enjoy uninterrupted panoramas of the landscape. To preserve the purity of this view, we tucked the outdoor living space off to the side, linking it to the kitchen and family room.

With its clear-cut outlook, the house delivers a unique message about how to respond to a site in a way that not only brings a richness to the design but also fosters a full family life inside. Achieving this takes both a rigorous approach as well as an extraordinary sense of intuition. With confidence in the process, I let my heart guide the design. This is the signature tool I bring to all my work.

PREVIOUS: Large expanses of glass at the second story help the house blend into the surrounding treetops.

RIGHT: A series of limestone piers and window openings at the entryway create a compositional moment that adds privacy even as it teases what's beyond. A strategic opening in the deep overhang above allows light to pour through to the plantings below. Barker Evans Landscape Design responded with compositions combining moments of color with minimalist hardscape.

LEFT: A floating wall adds space for the client's ever-expanding art collection—which includes work by Meredith Pardue, Julian Opie, and Mel Bochner, seen here—while providing privacy from the street.

Ellsworth Kelly

RIGHT: In the living room, the pattern of the lacquered panels above the fireplace mirrors the rhythm of the exterior piers and windows. Working with interior designer Travis Clifton, the homeowner found ways to connect the art collection and decor, such as placing artwork in unexpected places.

OVERLEAF: Glass extends beyond the edge of the living room, which has an easy but tailored attitude.

LEFT AND ABOVE: A collection of art, books, and objects on the coffee table brings color to the subdued palette. A work by Roy Lichtenstein is perched on a lacquered ledge near the fireplace.

OPPOSITE: An art-filled gallery that ends in open stairs is perfectly aligned with a magnificent tree just outside.

LEFT: A serving area behind the dining table acts as a ledge to support a constantly rotating selection of art.

BELOW: A small sculpture by Jeff Koons adds a pop of pink.

OVERLEAF: Built-in wall-to-wall seating anchors the kitchen's breakfast table, which is illuminated by a Tom Dixon pendant.

PAGE 233: A Boffi kitchen minimizes visual clutter from appliances and allows the eye to move to the view beyond.

RIGHT: With the pool and terrace tucked off to the side, views from the interiors are unobstructed by layers of outdoor furniture. A limestone wall extends from the house to define the thoughtfully furnished pool terrace.

OVERLEAF: The front facade is like a work of sculpture, with the screen wall creating an arresting visual play, especially in the evening, when the house is illuminated from within.

Acknowledgments

It may have begun in my bedroom with a collection of blankets and a flashlight—draped fabric, tucked in drawers, with safety-pinned structural supports—or perhaps it was the times outside when I wrapped leftover boards and branches around trees to create a hut. Somewhere in the chaos of building my early childhood forts, the passion to shape meaningful spaces was born. I am grateful to be able to realize my dream, in which facades are now made with elegant stone panels and windows look out onto landscape vistas. However, my passion is nothing without the richness that comes from the guidance and collaboration of others. Behind each design moment and chapter are the many talents who have surrounded me along the way.

ROBBINS ARCHITECTURE TEAM: Bringing these homes to life takes an almost inconceivable amount of talent and hard work. None of these projects could be realized without Robbins Architecture's incredible team of people, who each bring inspiration, art, and skill to everything they touch. I am grateful to share this journey with this group of funny, smart, and caring architects. Each design is a voice of many. Without them none of this could happen.

THE MEANINGFUL MODERN HOME TEAM: Jill Cohen—the team captain—who brought beauty, clarity, and direction, and who can walk into a room and see the pages of a book. Thank you for saying yes. Rita Sowins, who made the composition of this book feel effortless. You brought balance and serenity to each spread. Jacqueline Terrebonne, who skillfully crafted each story to share meaning over details. To Monacelli and my editor, Jenny Florence, who supported and understood the underlying principle of softness and strength.

ROGER DAVIES: I am forever grateful for your ability to capture the essence of our architecture and interiors. You brought so much more than a skillful composition and balanced lighting. Architecture is an experience. With each image you found a way to capture the soul of the space with richness, feeling, and nuance.

BERTA SHAPIRO: You taught me everything from the richness of layering to the sophistication of a found object. We each had our strengths, but because of you I learned how a house should live. Together we worked tirelessly—always with a tape measure—testing dimensions so that the abstract lines on the page were always brought back to "how-does-it-feel." A home is an intimate thing, and I am grateful for these early lessons.

MY CLIENTS: You challenge me, fill my soul, and become my friends. Together we shape a wish list into a home. A special thank-you to Erika Pearsall and Ned Jannotta, who gave me my first ground-up residential project on a site that architects dream of—at the foot of the Tetons. The marriage of nature and home began there.

NICK AND NATALIE: You taught me the richness of juggling school drop-offs with project deadlines, construction site visits with the Rainforest Cafe. With you at my side, your support and pride continue to fuel me. Special thanks, Natalie, for your writing skills, which have allowed my voice and design principles to be shaped into words. (I am sorry you had to edit even this!)

MOM AND DAD: My mother worked three jobs to put me through Cornell and set the example of leading with kindness. My father was an engineer and introduced me to the career of architecture. People questioned whether my expensive college would pay off: "She might get married and not make use of the degree." Thank you for believing in me. You gave me a love that no one can ever take away.

All photos by Roger Davies unless noted otherwise.

Cover, pp. 64–65, 162–63, and 173: Steve Hall, Hall+Merrick+McCaugherty
pp. 44, 61, and 66–67: Steve Freihon

Library of Congress Control Number: 2023930933

ISBN 978-1-58093-623-1

Design by Rita Sowins / Sowins Design

Printed in China

Monacelli
A Phaidon Company
65 Bleecker Street
New York, New York 10012
monacellipress.com

CREDITS

LAKESIDE MIDCENTURY
INTERIOR DESIGN: ROBBINS ARCHITECTURE
LANDSCAPE ARCHITECTURE: SCOTT BYRON & CO.

MOUNTAIN MODERN
INTERIOR DESIGN: SHAWN HENDERSON
LANDSCAPE ARCHITECTURE: HOERR SCHAUDT AND
    DESIGN WORKSHOP

HOME ON THE RANCH
INTERIOR DESIGN: BERTA SHAPIRO DESIGN

MIDWEST SANCTUARY
INTERIOR DESIGN: JANET MCCANN ASSOCIATES
LANDSCAPE ARCHITECTURE: MARIANI LANDSCAPE

WESTERN RETREAT
INTERIOR DESIGN: HERRINGBONE DESIGN
LANDSCAPE ARCHITECTURE: DESIGN WORKSHOP

INTO THE WOODS
INTERIOR DESIGN: ROBBINS ARCHITECTURE
LANDSCAPE ARCHITECTURE: SCOTT BYRON & CO.

MAKING WAVES
INTERIOR DESIGN: ROBBINS ARCHITECTURE
LANDSCAPE ARCHITECTURE: HOERR SCHAUDT

TRIBECA LOFT
INTERIOR DESIGN: MARY LUBY INTERIOR DESIGN

RAVINE RETREAT
INTERIOR DESIGN: T CLIFTON DESIGN
LANDSCAPE ARCHITECTURE: BARKER EVANS LANDSCAPE DESIGN

monacellipress.com

978 1 58093 623 1